From Broken To Healed

By Sonja Walker

A Woman's Journey Into The World & Her Path Back to Christ

No part of this publication may be reproduced, stored, or transmitted in any form or by any means, electronic, mechanical, photocopying, recording, scanning, or otherwise, except as permitted under Section 107 or 108 of the 1976 United States Copyright Act without the prior written permission of the author. Requests to the author or publisher for permission should be addressed to the following email:sonjab68@outlook.com.

Limit of liability/disclaimer of warranty:
While the publisher and author have used their best efforts in preparing this guide, they make no representation or warranties with respect to the accuracy or completeness of the contents of this document and specifically disclaim any implied warranties of merchantability or fitness for particular purpose. No warranty may be created or extended by sales representatives, promoters, or written sales materials.
The advice and strategies contained herein may not be suitable for your situation. You should consult with a professional where appropriate.

Neither the publisher nor the author shall be liable for any loss of profit or any other commercial damages, including but not limited to special, incidental, consequential, or other damages.
Copyright© 2021

Dedication

I would like to dedicate this book to my parents that raised me: Norman L. and Virgie M. Davis. Without giving it a second thought, they agreed to become my guardians / parents. They never had any children of their own together. But God knew that I was coming to them one day. So, He prepared a place and space in their hearts for me. They loved, raised and nurtured me as if I was their very own birth child. They are the only parents that I truly knew growing up. I will always love them, cherish and appreciate them for all they did for me. There are no words that can ever say what I feel in my heart for them as my parents. I am the woman I am and the person I am today because of them. Mom and Dad I love you and miss you more than you can know.

Your daughter forever,

Sonja Walker

Dedication continued....

A Letter to my Mother: Dorothy L. Walker,

I want you to know that I will always love you and respect you from the bottom of my heart. What love you must have for me to make the ultimate sacrifice and give up your only child. I don't know what it took for you to make that decision. I don't know the hurt or pain that it caused you to not have your child with you. What I do know is that only a mother with a special love for her child could do it. For many years I didn't understand why you didn't want me. But what I came to find out is that it was all a part of God's plan to give me the spiritual foundation that I would need now at this time in my life's journey. So, I say thank you for loving me more than life itself to send me where you knew I needed to be. Thank you for loving me so much that you were always there in a phone call or visit. Thank you for being the mother that I needed for the past 17 years and will still need until God says otherwise. I love and appreciate and respect you so much.

Love,

Your daughter,

Sonja Walker

Dedication continued........

Delma Fransaw, my sister, I thank God for giving me sister like you who I love, admire, trust, and can always go to for prayer. I know that we may not always see things eye to eye. However, I know even still now there are times your love reveals you are here for me and love me. It has been a joy in being your little sister. We have cried and laughed together. We have shared some struggles, tough times and a whole lot of memories together. Through all of it the best thing we have shared has been being sisters. I love you with all my heart. You are a great wife, mother, grandmother, aunt and best of ALL a sister. There would be no Sonja C. Walker without you!

Love,

Your Sister

Original Cover Designer: Willard E. Finerson III

Love,

Your Mom

Table of Contents

Introduction 1
Chapter 1: The Call 6
Chapter 2: The Prodigal Daughter's Bad Choices 11
Chapter 3: Mom 19
Chapter 4: God said ENOUGH!! 33
Chapter 5: The Suicide Attempt 37
Chapter 6: BUT GOD!! 52
Chapter 7: The Abuse 57
Chapter 8: The Pain 66
Chapter 9: The Healing 73
Chapter 10: The Ministry 90
Conclusion 100

Introduction

I was born on August 6, 1968 to the parents Eddie and Dorothy Walker of Chicago, IL. I lived with my parents until I was about 24 months old in Chicago. I don't remember anything about that time in my life. My parents at some point were no longer able to stay married.

My mom needed someone that could take care of me and raise me. At this point, my mother didn't feel that she would be able to care for me with all that was going on. So, she took me to Saint Louis, Missouri to her older sister and brother-in-law Virgie M. Davis and Norman L. Davis.

They agreed to keep me for a while until my mother could get things worked out in Chicago. However, she was still working things out when on August 1, 1971 it was determined by the Judge that I would legally be given to Virgie and Norman Davis. On that day they became my parents for Life.

They raised me in a loving home and environment. They spoiled me and gave me any and everything that I could have wanted, asked for and needed; as well as anything I didn't need.

They provided a model of both a mother and father in the same household together raising a child. They showed me about being married to one person until death do them part.

I learned what it was to have a father and mother's love for their child. They showed me how you love a child that is not yours by birth. They showed me the sacrifices that parents are willing to make for their child. There was always unconditional love from them for me, their daughter.

They are both gone now and I miss them dearly. My dad died when I was in high school. I was sixteen years old when my dad died. He wasn't with us when he died so I never got a chance to say good-bye and how much I loved him. That really hurt me. My mom died on July 7, 1992 at 7am in the morning 7/7/7: completion.

That hurt as well but in a different kind of way. My rock, my supporter, my believer (in me) was now gone. What's left of our family in this world is now only me. My mom got saved when I was six years old in 1974 and started attending the Pentecostal Church of God.

My mom was filled with the Holy Ghost the very night she got baptized at Lively Stone Pentecostal Church. This took place during a revival being preached by then, Evangelist E. Joshua. My mother was soon put to work on the pastor's aide, adult choir and then God called her to the ministry. My mother served in this capacity until she could no longer serve. At the age of six, on December 1974 right before Christmas during a revival I got saved. It was a Sunday night ending revival under then Pastor Gregory (who has passed on now). I got baptized that night and came upstairs. When I came upstairs my mom told me to go up for prayer. I was at the end of the prayer line and Pastor Gregory was making her way to the end but she asked me a question. She asked me did I want the Holy Ghost. She then prayed for me and I fell out speaking in tongues receiving the Holy Ghost.

I was trained up in the church under the power of the Holy Ghost. I was also trained in the areas of prayer fasting, and reading the word of God. During my time in church I taught Sunday school and sang in the Choirs (children's choir and the adult choir). I also worked with the Youth Department and was on the Usher Board. This was the beginning of my spiritual life.

Chapter 1: The Call

At the age of sixteen I knew that God had called to me to the ministry. I of course did not want any part of that at all. Answering the call of ministry meant going through those hard tests that you don't want to go through. I watched my mom Minister Virgie Davis go through some things in the ministry that, to me, were unimaginable.

I saw how she was treated by her family. I saw how she was hurt by her family. I just saw too much and said nope! No way! That is not for me at all! Being a minister, to me, meant that you have to suffer a lot. It meant going through those hard tests and trials. It meant, you know, trials, trials and more trials; the ones you want to avoid.

It meant not having any friends at all and always being about God's business. It meant having no business or life of your own. It meant there were some things I was going to have to give up. It meant a level of sacrifice I would have to yield and surrender to.

Answering the call (to ministry) required surrendering my will to the will of God. My life had to become his life. This was a type of sacrifice for ministry I was not willing to commit to at any age. I especially did not want to answer the call as a teenager. Nope! No way! Not happening!

However, being a minister was already in me and would come at unexpectant times. When it was time for my class to give the Sunday school review I would do it.

But I always ended up preaching the Sunday school review. I couldn't help it at all.

Every time it was my time I would say I am not going to preach at all. I'll just give it I thought. But you guessed it: that never happened. I kept preaching it every time. The saints at the church kept saying I was called to be a preacher. I would say "No I'm not"! God didn't tell me that at all!

Who was I to think that I could say no to the call of ministry because of my age? Jesus, at the age of twelve, was in the synagogue teaching and being about his Father's business. Could he say no because of his age? Absolutely Not! So, that right there confirms that age means nothing when you've been called by God!

I would constantly ask my mom, Minister (Min.) Virgie Davis if she knew what my calling was. Her answer to me first was always the question: "Don't you know what your calling is?" I would answer her back by saying "No I don't know what it is". That was not the truth.

I knew but I just did not want to admit it. I asked her again and this time she answered "yes I know what your calling is. Don't you?" I again answered "No". She said "Well, you need to ask him. I am not going to tell you." I said "Okay." My mother never told me. She took it to her grave.

So at the age of sixteen, until eighteen I would go to church but refuse to accept the call of God on my life. I didn't know that little by little I was beginning to rebel against God and his plans for me and my life. We will be moving on now to how I became the Prodigal daughter who walks away from God because of fear of her calling.

Chapter 2: The Prodigal Daughter's Bad Choices

What I can say about this is we all make bad choices at some point and time in our life. We may not think the choices are bad at the time. That is because we ignore all the signs and the things we see. Since I didn't want to be a minister at the age of nineteen, all the way until I was twenty-two years old, I decided to "do me" as the young people say. Well doing me didn't work like I thought it would.

Mom encouraged me to go to technical school. This was after I went to college but it didn't work for me after two tries. My very first bad choice came when I decided to date a young man, from my technical school. I had never dated before so I was thrilled that at age nineteen someone was interested in me.

So he asked me out on a date to my first concert: the group *Earth, Wind and Fire*. I didn't ask my mom about going on the date with the young man. I just told her I was going on a date. The young man took me to the concert. I ordered a rum and coke. I couldn't even drink it because I wasn't a drinker. I went to the clubs on the Eastside. My St. Louis people know what I'm talking about. I could dance but I still didn't fit in with the club scene. I started drinking on occasions; well that didn't work out either seeing I was a mean drunk.

We began dating but he really wasn't into me like I was him. I was in love, so I thought, with this young man. I began thinking if I could buy him things that he would love me. I also thought by buying him things his family would love me and that we would eventually get married. However, that never happened though.

I kept dating him although he wasn't dating me at all. I got to the point that I started drinking and going out more often. His friends and my friends kept trying to tell me that he was no good for me. I wouldn't listen to them or see the signs that were obviously right in front of my face. As time went on I started forging my mom's signature in checks and credit cards. I was buying stuff for him.

Sadly I was ever so wrong and again was still doing all the wrong things. I wasn't listening to God or any of the signs that were as big as red stop signs. Those are just a few of the bad choices that I made. There are too many to discuss them all, in this book. I am sharing the times that God has laid on my heart to share. I am also sharing what happens when God says enough is enough!

After dating the young man (that I started dating at age 19) for about 4 years, I discovered he was a down-low brother. God truly protected his prodigal daughter as he never wanted to do anything other than just go to concerts, clubs and out to eat. We were never intimate at all. He eventually broke up with me and I got mad with him.

That was God looking out for me even when I wasn't concerned for myself. Over these several years my life was a **HOT MESS!**

What advice can you give to women who want to buy a man's love?

In looking at my own life I would say that as a little girl I did not know my own identity. This is because at the age of two years old I was given to my aunt and uncle legally to be raised. That meant for the rest of my life I would wonder who I was. In not knowing who I was, I could not love myself, feel worthy of being loved and only knew rejection. Then those things followed me throughout my life of growing up into a teenager, a young lady and then a grown woman. Not knowing my identity, feeling rejected and having low self-esteem caused me to be easy prey for the wrong kind of men. So, know your identity and your own self-worth. That will keep you from trying to buy a man's love.

Seek God first to find out the root of why you keep trying to buy love from men. Then go to counseling if you can afford it to get the professional help in unpacking those same things.

You must find out why you feel that buying a man's love is the only way to be loved. After you start finding that out, then begin to ask God to teach you how to love Him. As you learn to love God you will begin to learn how to love yourself since God is love. The scripture I John 4:8 tells us that we do not love because we do not know God and He is Love. Once you love yourself then you will be able to love others. At which point you will know that you are worthy of someone loving freely and not because you brought them with things in order for them to love you.

Advice to women who want to buy their child's love.

You cannot buy your child(ren's) love. It is not real love if they only love you for the things that you get them. What happens when you are unable to buy them things anymore? What happens when the things just go away because of life circumstances happened and they can't be replaced by you? You must show child(ren) that you love them without buying material things. However, to do that you must love yourself first. That means once again it goes back to asking God to teach you how to love Him. So that you can be taught how to love yourself and then your child(ren).

Women who want to buy their family and friend's love.

It is the same principle for family and friends as anything else. It all goes back to God. What I mean by that is you must first know God and ask Him to teach you how to love Him. Once you really know how to do that, He can begin working on you. Then you are able to love yourself so that you can love others. Loves starts at home and then spreads around that is the old saying. However, according to scripture Mark 12:31, we are to love others as we love ourselves.

Chapter 3: Mom

As a nurturer my mom was wonderful. She would do and give me any and everything that I needed, wanted and things that I did not want or ask for at all. I would say because she never had any children of her own, she overdid it with me. I was spoiled rotten and at the time I know to her it seemed like a good thing, but it was not.

When I was little we would get dressed up and go shopping all day on Saturday, we would eat breakfast lunch and dinner at restaurants all day before we came home. We would be with people she knew from church. I loved shopping. We would go to the mall and the grocery store. We would go to the Wellston Loop's Woolworth store. We would also shop at JC Penney and then we would go back home. We would also go to

Northwest plaza when it was an outdoor mall. We would shop and go to Dillard's and Boyd's men's clothing store. They also had a Woolworth out there so we would shop there too.

We also took vacations. In the summer of 1973 we went to California to Disneyland. That was our first airplane trip as a family. We stayed in a hotel that was right across from Disneyland. However, during our trip there the devil first tried to take my life at the age of five. I was stricken with a fever and tonsillitis. The doctors told my parents to bathe me in ice cold water to break the fever. My mom couldn't do it so my dad did it even though I was hollering and screaming. I took Tylenol and the fever was broken and I was able to go back to Disneyland. My aunt, my mom's sister (aunt

Maxine) lived and worked in California. We got to see her and spend time with her. We flew back home and I had to have my first surgery at the age of five to have my tonsils removed.

My mom spent the night at the hospital with me. Then she told my biological mom and she came to the hospital so I had both of them at the hospital. My dad also came two days later when he was able to get off of work. In the summer of 1977 we went to Atlanta Georgia and we went to a church convention and we went to Six Flags over Georgia. That would have been the second to last trip I took with my mom. I then took another trip with my dad at age ten to his hometown of Little Rock Arkansas. On the road to Arkansas I almost choked on a peppermint. Dad had to pull over and he kept hitting my back until I coughed the peppermint up. When I was 12 my mom and I went to Eureka Springs Arkansas and we went to a live outdoor play. It was a play about Christ being crucified. We also took a family trip to Lawrence Kansas to visit my mother's oldest sister and we went shopping and had a picnic. One of the places my parents wanted to go but were not able to take me was Niagara Falls, Canada. My mother prayed for me a lot. She kept me in church even when I did not want to go. She would have my sister come and get me as I did not have a license yet and she had become blind. My mother was a diabetic when I was a freshman in high school. She went to dialysis for many years. By the time I was a junior in high school is when the diabetes began to take her eyesight. She was legally blind in one eye and was losing sight in the other. I remember at age 10 dad had a heart attack while I was home with him. I kept calling my mom and she rushed him 30 minutes away to the hospital. He was pronounced dead twice on the table! My mom was praying for him and she had the church praying. They brought dad back to life and he developed Alzheimer's. Because of the oxygen he lost in his brain the doctors said he would deteriorate. However, he was fine until I was age 14. When I turned 14 dad would then deteriorate and he did not remember who he was. I had to stay with relatives for a while because of his memory loss. I was afraid to stay at our house because dad busted out a window looking for his keys which were in his pocket. Sometime after that, dad called his family in Arkansas and he told them to come and get him. He cried and said he loved us and he had to go and he left with them. I believe dad knew he was dying so he went back to his birth home. Six months after he went back to his hometown in Arkansas he died. He died due to complications of diabetes. Gained green set into his toe and spread all through his body. For me that was hard because there was no closure. I never had a chance to say goodbye. Daddy was big on telling me to never let a man put his hands on me. He was a former MP in the army and had a gun but he never used it. He was a good cook and he was always making homemade pancakes and cornbread from scratch. Dad was a protector. He loved my mom and my older sister and me. Couldn't anybody mess with his wife and kids! He did not play that!

Mom taught me how to pray and fast and read the Bible. She would give me words of wisdom. I would not listen to her sometimes. Other times I would not listen. I regret not listening.

My parents did not have any arguments that I remember until they were sick. They were a great example of an until death do us part couple. This was mom's first marriage but it was dad's fourth marriage. He said mom was the one and he never looked back.

Mom would tell me to watch how you treat people because the way you treat them is the way they would treat you. In other words, you teach people how to treat you. My mom loved me unconditionally.

Mom was not a big talker. It's not that mom said a lot but her actions spoke a lot to me. She had a strong work ethic. She worked until she couldn't work anymore. Mom was about helping other people. Her actions prevailed and she was a prime example of being a good wife when you know your husband is sick. Mom protected me when I should have gone to jail for some of the things that I did back then. My mother impacted me for the call. She had great faith. Even as a diabetic on dialysis and going blind she was still determined to help and stand in the gap for others. She had a great grace. She experienced several mini heart attacks. Every time this happened, they would count her out. However, she would come right back. She became an inspiration to her own doctors. One of her doctors was a kidney specialist and other was a heart specialist. One of the doctors said he just stopped counting her out because he knew she would bounce back. He just waited to see what she would do. She had such a great faith to keep fighting! There were times when her sugar was low that she didn't know who anyone was. However, her faith and strong relationship with God was still strong! She could sing and pray. She would sing "If I could just help somebody then I know my living would not be in vain." I can hear her singing that song right now! She could pray and knew her word and revelation of the word. These things about her profoundly impacted me for the call. She would always keep me in church, rooted and grounded. She was a living epistle of the scripture "train up a child". Although I did not always make it easy for her she allowed me to answer the call. That's why I can do what I do now in ministry. She knew I was a minister. I now know that she knew.

She just kept right on praying and believing God would draw me back. I was a horrible daughter during these years and my mom paid the financial price when she could have said "no let her go to jail to learn a lesson". A mother's God given unconditional love would not do that to her daughter. I wasted a lot of years that I can never ever get back. She loved me even when I had stolen her credit cards, forged her name, bought appliances, rented cars and stole her checks. She loved me when I took checks out of her check books, wrote check for cash, in her name and maxed them out. Even when I was mean and not a good daughter to her she still loved me anyway and prayed for me. When she could have prosecuted me she didn't. She paid off the debt that I owed. When I was prosecuted for a bad check to Enterprise leasing for a rental car, she could have walked away and she did not. She loved me, prayed for and encouraged me and told me that it would be alright. Just like Jesus dropped the charges of our sins with his love and his blood. Even when we were yet sinners and unwilling to surrender to him, he paid the ultimate price.

My other family members got angry but my mom never got angry. Mom had a strong grace for me. You just knew she loved me just by her actions. Her love would fight for me and defend me. Her love reminds me of how Jesus intercedes and stands in the gap for us. Even with my suicide attempt she still never got angry through it all! It was in this season, my mother, being a minister would pray and war for me, her daughter warrior. She would also get others to pray and stand in the gap for me as well. She kept fighting for me although the daughter she raised had become HOT MESS! The following page is a picture of mom and dad before I was born.

Willard Finerson,III, Dorothy Walker & Yours Truly

Chapter 4: God said ENOUGH!!

At age twenty-two God stepped in and said ENOUGH!! You've done things your way long enough, now we're going to do things my way. You've run from the call and your destiny and purpose long enough. We will now start doing things my way. I will start by getting your attention now.

So I got into some major trouble and committed a felony crime all in the name of love, stupidity; whatever you want to call it. I forged my mom's signature for checks for over $200. The company called my mom and asked her about it and she said she didn't write it.

The company filed papers against me to charge me with forgery. The warrants were out on me and I had to turn myself in. The only thing that she could do was pray for me that God would work it out. I went to court for the felony charge that I had and my pastor went with me to the court.

Pastor Coleman talked to me about doing things God's way. He encouraged me to seek the Lord to make sure that I knew that I was called to the ministry. Pastor Coleman spoke with me about getting back into church and being active and serving God. When we got to my Public Defender he was overwhelmed with all of the cases that he had.

The prosecutor was on a mission. She was definitely in no mood to make deals with anyone at all. I was facing serious jail time for what I had done. There was no way this time that my mom could get me out trouble. God had taken me out of my mom's hands and put me in His hands now.

When God wants you, He comes to get you no matter what you're doing, or where you are at. Pastor Coleman prayed with me about the situation and asked God to give me favor with both the prosecutor and the judge.

My Public Defender went to the prosecutor and said that if she makes restitution and does probation would she be willing to accept that? As this was taking place in the courtroom Pastor Coleman and I were outside in the hallway watching other people being told by their lawyers that they have to do some jail time because of their long record.

The Public Defender came back out to me and said that both the prosecutor and the judge will accept your deal of restitution and probation! God worked and moved in my favor.

I actually only ended up with nine months of probation because of my good behavior and paid the restitution off so quickly. I was let go on my own recognize agreeing to come back to court. I was able to go home that day! Praise God!

Chapter 5: The Suicide Attempt

During this time my mom Min. Virgie Davis was a prayer warrior back then. She kept praying to God and talking to my God sister about me and the things I was doing. My mom never gave up on me although the daughter she raised was an entire **HOT MESS!** She loved me unconditionally.

She loved me unconditionally but hated the sin I was in. Mom just kept right on praying and believing that God would draw me back. Mom protected me when there were times that I should have gone to jail. She paid the financial price. However, she could have said "No! Let her go to jail to learn her lesson." A mother's God given unconditional love would not allow her do that to her daughter. I was a horrible daughter during these years and I am not proud of it at all. There were years that were wasted by me. There were years that I could never get back again! I doubted myself so I thought. This was all because I didn't want to accept my call to ministry. I went to some dark places during this time. I went to places that I never thought that I would go to in my life. No one could have ever told me that I would visit these dark places in my life.

I was devastated after realizing all the hurt and damage I caused my mother. I couldn't take it anymore. I was afraid of going to jail and being turned out by other women. I didn't want to go to jail because I would lose my freedom, the devil bringing all of these thoughts and more to my head. He would tell me that nobody loves you. They won't forgive you and they hate you. God doesn't love you and He won't forgive you. It's too late for you, it's over now. Your life is over now. Then the enemy told me everyone would be better off if you just take your life. You won't hurt your mom anymore and it will all be better if you just die.

I attempted suicide at the age of 22 by taking all of my mom's diabetic pills at one time. I left her a suicide note apologizing to her for all I had done to her. I told her that I was sorry for all of the bad things that I've done and I needed to be gone so I wasn't a problem to her anymore. She had called the EMT's for herself because she wasn't feeling good. The ambulance came to see about my mom. But God sent them for me and they found the suicide note. They asked my mom some questions and she didn't know anything at all. While there they discovered my note they asked her about it. She told them that she didn't know anything about it because she was blind and couldn't see. The EMT's asked me how many pills I took. But because I was almost in a diabetic coma I couldn't answer them.

They asked my mom if the medication was hers that I took. I believe she told them yes. They then began to immediately work on me and take me to the hospital. I was taken to the hospital and my stomach was pumped. At that moment I had decided that I didn't want to die.

As one of my mom's caregivers I knew exactly how much of her diabetic medication that I needed to take in order to die. So what I did was take about thirty to forty pills of her diabetic medication.

I was age twenty two when this happened to me. I went to the ER where they began to pump my stomach to get the medication out of my system. While there I heard the nurse say "she is twenty two years old and attempted suicide. What could be so bad that she would want to end her life? She is such a young thing! Life is that bad she wants to do that?" During this time I began to tell God that I didn't want to die but I wanted to live. At that moment I decided that I would agree to going to the psychological ward for suicide watch. But once I got there I changed my mind and decided to go home. I got violent and upset about having to stay there. They called the orderlies to come and restrain me if I didn't calm down. I told them that I was not going to take that medication. They told me once I calmed down they would let me call my mom. I told my mom to call

Pastor Coleman and have him to call me. I still wouldn't take the medication. I told them they were trying to poison me with that medication. I kept saying it over and over again.

Pastor Coleman called and talked to the staff first and then Pastor Coleman asked them if he could talk to me. Pastor Coleman said "The medicine is not going to hurt you it's just to help you sleep". Pastor Coleman asked me to talk to the staff so that I could go home. He said "Sonny take the medicine for me please". I did what Pastor Coleman told me. I took the medicine and cooperated with the staff. I was able to sleep. I went to all of the group meetings while on the floor. Asst. Pastor Sutherlin bought me a Bible to read and prayed with, me. I appreciated this and read the Bible more than I did anything else. While I was in there God took me to Matthew 22:14: "For many are called but few are chosen." God let me know you are now in place to hear me and what I have to say about you and ministry. The following Sunday, a week later after my suicide attempt, I was allowed to go to the church for a few hours. Pastor Dickson preached that morning and after an altar call she prayed for me and said "God saw your heart and that you didn't want to die and spared your life ". After two weeks in the hospital I was allowed to go home!

Why most people commit suicide?

I believe that most people commit suicide because of spirit of rejection abandonment, and depression. The spirit of rejection is one that comes to oppress you and gives mental pressure and distress. In case you did not know, this spirit does not come from God but the enemy. People that have been rejected feel as though there is no one who wants them. They feel like there is not anybody that will love them for whatever season. This leads them to believe that there is no reason for living at all. They feel the things done are too bad for there to be self-love or love from others. There is also a spirit of abandonment that makes people feel like there must be a reason why they have been left to feel all alone in this world. Finally, you begin to have a spirit of depression, despair and despondency that causes a person to think that there is only one way out the situation or problem. They feel like there is no other way to get rid of the pain, hurt, rejection and abandonment and to be free. All these spirits will speak to them and cause the people to believe that suicide is the only answer or way out.

Why do people have the desire to commit suicide?

How many people probably regret suicide? What alternatives can take place other than suicide being the last result? Should someone write an action plan if the strong urge and desire to commit suicide comes over them? What kind of prayer declaration / paragraph can be prayed for those contemplating suicide?

There are spirits of rejection and abandonment that are behind the spirit of suicide. I say this because as I look back over my life now, I felt all those things about the trouble I had gotten into. The root of the spirit of rejection came from the fact that I felt like my biological parents did not want me. My biological father did not want me because my biological mother no longer wanted to be in the marriage. So because my biological mother did not want him she filed for divorce because of his cheating. As for my biological mother I felt like she did not want me either because she did not love me. I believe the reason she did not love me was because of her anger for my biological father at time. Then there were the feelings of abandonment that came from my biological parents as well all due to their divorce. As I grew older that then turned into bitterness toward them and my life's situation. Those spirits eventually would become the driving force behind many choices I would make in my life unknowingly. Once I got into trouble I did not see any way out. I believed no one loved me, no one cared about me and everyone was mad at me. Those spirits lead into the spirit of suicide which most times leads to death. The main spirit behind both these spirits is the spirit of rejection.

I would say that there are many people who have attempted suicide like me. Afterwards, they have regretted the decision of trying to take their own life. I also feel there are those who did succeed at taking their life who had second thoughts at the time it was happening. However, at the time they were not able to stop it from happening. I also feel there are those that even though they regret it and survive suicide, they still think about it and will probably attempt it again. Why? Because the same issues, problems, circumstances, or situations are still there. They have not been able to seek the right assistance with resolution to the hurt. For them to keep being a survivor they need to have the tools to help them find out what the root problem is that caused them to attempt suicide.

That is why I feel counseling or therapy is so important. Counseling and therapy is critical in discovering the root of why a person attempts suicide. You cannot find out why the person did commit suicide if they are gone and there is no note left behind to explain it. Find someone that you trust to talk with about what is going on inside of your mind. If you know how to call on the name of Jesus, just call on Him. Go to your doctor, pastor, or loved one and tell them "Hey I am having these kinds of thoughts in my mind and I need help". If those people will not listen or ignore you then go to someone else. Just keep going until you find someone that will listen and help you. There is someone or somebody that God has who will listen to you and will help you. One of the major stronghold spirits that pressures a person to commit suicide is the spirit of defeat. If you know someone that has attempted suicide, please bind the spirit of defeat and encourage them and help them know their worth.

There should be an action plan of what you need to do first when the thoughts of suicide come to you. Your written action plan needs to be somewhere you can find quickly. Most of us have cell phones. Therefore the action plan should be on our phone in the memo or note section. I would say pray and call on God to help you. If you cannot or do not know how to pray just say His name "Jesus". Then say "Lord Intervene". He will hear you and come and rescue you. You should have the National Suicide Prevention Lifeline number 1-800-273-8255. They are there to help you. You need to also have their website: *suicidepreventionlifeline.org* . Keep the website near you or in your phone as well. They have a lot of good information that can help you. Next you need to have a list of people you trust that you can call and talk to right away. All of this should be in your phone where you can find quickly. You also need to have it written down and hanging somewhere so that it can be seen and reached quickly.

This is a prayer that can be prayed:

"Lord God I do not want to die, I want to live. I am sorry for what I have done. God, I need you to help me right now! God, please help me! I have no place to go. I

do not feel like I have anyone to help me. God, please send someone to help me. I need you God. I declare that you are Jesus and Lord. I believe in my heart that you were raised from dead by God. I believe this in my heart that I am made right with you God. I declare my faith in you and that I am saved. In Jesus' Name. Amen." I prayed this after I had been in the mental ward for a week after surviving my attempt of suicide.

Chapter 6: BUT GOD!!

All that I can say is when it comes to talking about my consequences from committing a felony crime; that ultimately got expunged from my record God is a miracle worker! Pastor Coleman talked to me about doing things God's way. He also told me to seek God and make sure that I was called into the ministry. Pastor Coleman also spoke to me about getting back in church and serving God with my whole heart. Over the course of the next three years, my life began to change for the better. I gave my life back to God and got things right with my mom. She forgave and I apologized over and over for the things that I had done to her! Even with my suicide attempt she still never got angry through it all! I was able to get back on the usher board at church, work with the youth department and sing back in the choir once again. I was attending church services more and more now. I was building my relationship back up with God. I was constantly working good temp jobs through Kelly services. The assignments were always long ones and good ones. I was never without a job long. During this time I didn't think anything could go wrong now. God had forgiven me.

I'm being blessed now really good. However, things would soon change and change quickly. Now I am going to talk about how I fell into the cycle of doing well, then getting into messes, challenges, getting in and back out of the toxic relationships or behaviors.

The reason I kept having this same cycle is because of the spirit of rejection that I had from my childhood.

Since I did not know who I was as child I kept trying to find love in all the wrong places. When you are insecure, you have no idea about your identity. Insecurity causes you to look for love in all the wrong places. I also did not know my worth and had low self-esteem: a recipe for disaster in my life. Now all of that caused me to pick all the wrong men to date in my life. Notice that I said, ME doing the picking and never God.

I would repent and ask God to help me get out of these relationships that were no good for me. Then I would get back on track with my spiritual walk with God. I would be doing great and someone I know gets engaged and here I go back down that rabbit trail with the issues I listed a couple of sentences back. Then I would pray again and repent and get my life back on track with God. So, this never-ending cycle would go on for many years until one day I just got tired and wanted to be delivered and healed.

If you would have asked me back then if there was a restlessness in my soul the answer from me would have been no. But now, looking back over that time period in my life yes, it would be that I had a restless soul. Why? The answer to that is I had no real and true relationship with God. I did not know Him for myself. I did not know how to experience Him in an intimate and personal way. I will say it again; you must know your identity to keep from going down that path or cycle that keeps you bound with a restless soul. Although for some people there may have been church that caused them to go into the cycles that I just spoke about. However, for me the church was not to blame at all. I suffered from a spirit of rejection that led into other spirits.

Chapter 7: The Abuse

Another bad choice happened in my thirties. I had gotten back in church but was very lonely. I wanted a family of my own. So, I called this dating hotline and met the man who would become my children's father. He seemed like a nice man and appeared to love me a lot like I did him. He was everything that I thought I wanted in a man. He was tall, dark and handsome, sexy and could cook. It didn't matter to me that he wasn't saved and wasn't going to church. He believed in God and had a good job. He was the head cook of a restaurant. I fell in love with his family and they seemed to have done the same with me. Things were going well except he did not have a good relationship with his family until we got together. He hated his mother and father and was mean to them. He would mistreat them. I would say something to him about it and it would stop. So, here I thought I was changing him. NOT! I was only being deceived by what I wanted to see. Within two years of our relationship I got pregnant with our first child, a daughter, Melanie Evonne Finerson.. She was born on November 2, 2000. She passed away two days later on November 4, 2000. This caused a strain on our relationship but we got passed it. Then in December 2001 I became pregnant again with our second child, Willard Earl Finerson III.

One day I had enough of the relationship. He threatened to kill my son and me! He pushed me and threw a D.V.D. player at me. If I hadn't ducked it would've hit me and killed me. That was all it took. My son and I left him and never looked back again. At this point our relationship was really over and we went our separate ways. I carried a lot of hate, anger and resentment towards him for all of the pain and hurt that he caused in my life. I felt like this was my punishment for treating my mom so badly during those 3 years. I stayed even when I saw the abuse because I wanted my son to have a mother and father in the household.

In all of this I found out this man was not divorced. He was still married! Wow! What a blow and shock that was to me.

After this I had a couple more bad choices in men, still looking for love in all the wrong places and people. In reference to these two relationships, again and again I thought they were who God wanted me to be with and marry.

You have to accept the fact that you are being abused in a relationship. A lot of people are in denial they are being abused. The person in denial says they know but they have an excuse for the abuser and an excuse to stay. Then there is the woman who knows she is being abused but feels that abusive love or treatment is better than no love or treatment at all!

The last kind of woman is the one who knows they are being abused but believe they are the one who can change the abuser. These are all 3 different women but they are all one in the same because they are all looking for love in all the wrong places. These women share the same common denominator. This common denominator is they do not know how to love themselves. They are looking for external love instead of internal. It is ok to seek or have external love but if you seek it first before internal, there will always be a deficit. The reason I was impatient was because I wanted a family, so I accepted the first man that came along. Now mind you he wasn't the man that God sent, he was the man that I chose. He was everything I wanted: tall, dark and handsome. I thought I could change him. Why do you think women think they can change a man? For me I would say that because we feel we are that one and we have the strongest personality. I wanted affection and I wanted to be like the Joneses. I wanted to fit in. Everybody else had someone so I wanted what they had. I wanted acceptance. The best advice I can give to women is what I have learned:

Learn to love yourself by learning to love God and allowing God to love you. We have to learn to allow God to love us because some of us have been so rejected by others we can't even believe a God so big can love us with no strings attached! I learned to depend on God because there was nowhere else to turn. I cried out and asked God if you be real then show up for me. That's where the journey to prayer begun. The more I was seeking God the more I became content. I focused on my son and God and school. I went back to school to get my degree in Business Administration and Information Technology. I also focused on ministry. Once I added these things to my life I became content.

Healing and building your self-esteem is crucial. The healing process is never over and is a continual journey. You have to allow God to do surgery on your heart emotionally in order to remove the things that cause the pain and the rejection and the hurt. As you heal, your self-esteem increases. You begin to heal yourself as God sees you.

I began to love myself and date myself which took my mind off of wanting to be married. What do I mean by dating myself? You dress up and go to a nice restaurant and eat by yourself and you enjoy it. You go to the movies. You take a trip. You spend time getting to know you. There is such a thing as getting to know yourself or just enjoying your own company. My fear was lack of companionship. I never had a fear of being alone by myself, just me and my conscious. But some of you may have the issues with being alone by yourself. You cannot be afraid of your thoughts because that is the only way you get to know who you are. I believe that dating yourself is the only way to find out what you do want and what you don't. Dating yourself allows you to discover what you are willing to accept and allow. Having girlfriends also allows you to take your mind off of not being married. Your words can change your atmosphere. The following are powerful affirmations I love that have helped build my faith and confidence.

It says:

God says you are unique: Psalm 139:13 special Ephesians 2:10 lovely Daniel 12:3, precious I

Corinthians 6:20, Strong Psalm 18:35, Chosen John 15:16, Forgiven, Psalm 103:12.

Michelle Obama said "being healthy is not just getting on a scale and measuring your waistline. We need to be clear about how we fell and how we feel about ourselves". W.EB. Dubois said "there is no force equal to a woman determined to rise".

Chapter 8: The Pain

The pain I suffered after losing my mom Virgie Davis on July 7, 1992 was overwhelming. My life was never the same again. Then pain of losing my daughter Melanie Evonne Victoria Finerson on November 4, 2000 was all too much for me. I've carried the guilt, hurt and pain of what I did to my mom around with me for that last 25 years. I've carried the hurt and pain of losing my daughter for the last 17 years. I carried the pain, rejection, and hurt from my son's father for 3 years. I've carried this around for so long. This is because I felt and thought this was God's punishment to me for all of the bad things that I had done in my life to my mom. I thought it was His punishment for me, having children without being married. So, I thought that I was just supposed to carry it all around with me. So I did carry it around with me.

There are all kinds of hurt: physical, mental, spiritual, and emotional pain I've had to encounter. But we have all encountered pain in our lives. Sometimes we have had to bear various levels of pain all at the same time. For example in a relationship you can be abused physically and it hurts emotionally and it can break your spirit. Sometimes it is hard to get over the devastation of the hurt that has occurred in our life.

In this chapter I want to talk more about the emotional hurt that we go through which takes longer for us to get over. The toll of the emotional hurt that happens in our life will sometimes cause us to give up on people, life, and everything that we know. This pain can also cause us to give up on God. Why is that you might ask? It is because we are emotional beings that have been created by God. I also contribute it to the fact that it is hard to wrap our head around the fact anyone or anything could ever hurt us in such a way that it causes us to want to die or give up on life. The reason hurt continues to grow is because we have not actually grieved for the situation that has caused us the hurt and pain.

I would also say that the number one thing above all else is that we must want to break covenant with hurt. So, in this chapter we are going to talk about how to break covenant from or with hurt. First of all we need to know what covenant is in order to break away from it. Covenant is an agreement with something or someone. In other words, we have come into agreement with being hurt and having pain in our lives and situations. That is NOT what God is calling for us to have covenant with in our lives. No. God is asking us to be in covenant with Him and His word that is spoken to and over us.

However, you cannot do that if you are not in a place where you can truly hear from God. In order to break covenant from hurt and pain we must first recognize we have come into covenant with both the hurt and the emotions of pain. This is hard for us to do because we feel as though we are not in agreement with either of those things at all. For me this would mean admitting that I had made a mistake, fallen into sin and that I am in a bad situation. What I discovered was that I had to admit and accept the fact I had been hurt and there was pain involved. I also came to realize I had to forgive myself before I forgive others.

The next thing that I needed to do was to forgive those people that cause the hurt and pain in my Life. I needed to know that forgiveness was not for the other person, but it was for me. The longer you hold onto unforgiveness, the longer the other person has a hold on you. That person still has control over your life. There is also deliverance and inner healing that needs to be done as well.

Hurt kept me stuck because I allowed it to become rooted in me and made it a part of my make-up. That hurt becomes a root that is the spirit of rejection which then becomes the branch spirit of bitterness. That branch leads into another spirit called abandonment.

When we have all of these branches growing we become stuck in that moment, space and place of hurt and devastation. After we get stuck there it will lead us into denial that there is nothing wrong at all. We will just go and say that we are healed and fine although we still need to be delivered. Then we start doing things that are sinful and start to wonder why we are doing those things. Not considering that I have masked over the hurt and pain that it was causing me to sin. The hurt can turn into a spirit of infirmity. Now I had all kinds of sickness in my body. Hurt drew me to healing when I found that there was nothing else left. I discovered that man could not take it away since he was the one who caused the hurt. In that moment I realized that I could not wish it or make it go away. I was then willing and ready for freedom. I was at a point in my life where I said, "God if you be real please come and do this for me." It was at that point I began pursuing God because I did not know what else to do. In the next chapter I will discuss how I went from being broken to being healed today.

Chapter 9: The Healing

WOW!! The healing began in January 2017 when I went to a life changing conference called "Fire Conference 2017". My god sisters and I went with the expectation that God was going to do some GREAT things for us at this conference. That is exactly what happened! God did some GREAT and AMAZING things that weekend at the conference! It changed me so much that I've not been the same!

There was a big knot that had been on my back for the last fourteen years. The knot was a result of an epidural needle administered after giving birth to my son. It was there but never painful. The pain only began when God started healing me from it. Often times we want to be healed but do not wat to go through pain necessary for healing process to be competed. Once I endured the pain the healing began! God started the process of healing it and it is now gone! During this conference God also began to heal me from the hurt, pain and rejection. God began to deliver me from the rejection of my biological father not wanting to be a part of my life at all.

On March fifth my god sister called me and said that God showed her in a vision during her prayer time that I had a lot of Life Toxins in my body that were making me sick. She told me that I needed to have someone I trust to pray over me for deliverance. On April 30th, my other god sister prayed over me. She told me that God wanted to heal me of my life's hurts, pain, guilt and rejection. That God was going to use everything that I had been through to help other ladies. She told me the things I had been through I only survived with God's help. My experiences would have caused some other folks to not have their life or to give up. She shared how God was going to give me compassion and joy. She told me that I had to let my mom and daughter go and that it was okay to let them go. She said that I could still love them and keep them in my heart. She told me that the tears I shed now from sorrow are going to turn into tears of joy. She said that the process was going to be ugly at times. But if I followed the process God was going to heal me. So, I chose to get the courage to trust the process. Therefore, I am able to stand here before you today and share my testimony.

How healing takes place over time, not instantaneous

In this chapter I am also going talk about how my bitterness and anger have caused me physical, emotional and spiritual sickness. I will also share how it has caused me to hurt those closest to me. These people are who God has sent to be my family, and to cover and protect me. I am currently a part of a leadership fellowship in which I am learning so much about spirits that caused me to be in the condition that I was in some areas of my life. It is helping me to see the current areas where I am still in a condition(s) that needs much more deliverance in order for me to be healed.

I am going to look at deliverance first and what God gave me about it. The next thing that I will talk about will be the healing that shall come after the deliverance. What I want you to know most importantly is that it all takes work. It is not something that you will get or attain overnight or instantly. It is something that you must allow time and patience for God to deal with and walk you through it. There are specific individuals God will allow to walk through it with you. They are your Peter, James, and John that God gives to you. They are ones who will cover and protect you on this journey through deliverance into healing.

We all need deliverance and healing. It is for everyone that is seeking and asking God for it. We cannot and should not think just because we are Christians that we do not need to be delivered and healed. God knows that we need to be healed and delivered. He is just waiting on us to surrender our will to His will. God is just waiting on us to say "God I need you to deliver and heal me. God, I want to be delivered and healed."

A lot of times we believe that if I just keep pushing past whatever caused me to be broken and shattered I will just be okay. However, that is not true at all. Simply pushing through pain only leads to more destructive behavior and habits. This makes it hard or next to impossible to break these issues on our own. You must admit to the fact that you are broken and shattered. You must come to terms with the fact that you need to be delivered and healed to move to what God has for you. There is a process to being delivered and healed that we all must go through if we want to be made whole and healed from brokenness.

What is deliverance? "The state of being released, set free, rescued." (Thomas Chain Reference Bible). You must know that when it comes to deliverance there will be and is a level of F.E.A.R. (**F**alse **E**vidence **A**ppearing **R**eal). It will keep you from wanting or being delivered. It will often hold you hostage and keep you stagnant. I like that two of the words in the definition for deliverance are SET FREE!! The devil wants you to believe that there is no need for deliverance. He also wants you to be afraid of being delivered and SET FREE!! It is a powerful thing when God sets you FREE!!

There were two scriptures that God gave me about healing that I want to share right now. The first one is PSALM 34:4 "I sought the Lord, and He heard me, and delivered me from all my fears." So, the scripture tells us that we should not be afraid and that we should seek Him to be delivered from fear. The second scripture is PSALM 107:6 "Then they cried out to the Lord in their trouble; and He delivered them out of their distresses." As we see in these two scriptures in the book of Psalm we can be delivered from the fear, trouble, and stress in our lives. Deliverance must be something that you want from God for there to be healing.

God showed me that there was something that I had never seen before in the word Healthy. I would like to share with you what it was that He showed me after I had gotten healed. Get a piece of paper and write the word Healthy on it (leave space between each letter).

Now after you have done that cover up the last three letters of the word. What do you have? **HEAL.** Are you surprised to see that word? Yep, I was too. I had never noticed that the word Heal was in the word Healthy. How many times have you looked at the word Healthy and never noticed that the word **Heal** was in it? So that means God wants us to be healed in order to be healthy. God wants us to be healthy Spiritually, Physically, Emotionally and Mentally.

There is a scripture that God led me to. This scripture assures me that I do not have to be broken or remain broken. It also assures me that He wants to make me whole and that He wants to mend my wounds. It is PSALM 147:3 "He heals the brokenhearted and binds up their wounds." Here we see that the Lord will heal our broken hearts and covers up our wounds. So, there is no reason for us to walk around broken and wounded.

For there to be both deliverance and healing there must be Faith. What is the dictionary's definition of Faith? Webster's online dictionary defines faith as: "1. Allegiance to duty or a person, 2. Belief and trust in and loyalty to God., 3. Firm belief in something for which there is no proof., 4. Something that is believed especially with strong conviction." This is what we have to get deliverance and healing. In the scripture HEBREWS11:1 KJV "Now faith is the substance of things hoped for, the evidence of things not seen." It lets us know that we must believe it even though we might not see it right away. There is deliverance and healing coming if we trust and believe God. We must be **F**ully **A**nticipating **I**t **T**o **H**appen and **F**orever **A**lways **I** **T**rust **H**im these both equal **FAITH!!**

After I had gotten my deliverance that meant that I needed healing from God. See, I could have just been delivered by God and not healed. That would not have been good or worked at all. Why? In order to move on with the will of God I had to be healed. Healing is not the same for everyone and looks different for everyone. The only thing that is the same is the fact that we all must be delivered, healed and that it can only come from God. It does not come from man but from Him. Now God uses man to do the healing, yes that is true. But if not for God then man would not be able to heal people. Healing for me was that I needed to be delivered from things in my past and present. What I am discovering is that both deliverance and healing is an ongoing process that never ends. There may be intermission periods to where God is balancing your life in order to maximize your potential. There are other periods where other areas can be rooted out. Then when there is a significant amount of areas that have been rooted out it is imperative to occasionally for the purpose of maintenance to receive deliverance regardless of your title. God always looks at the heart, soul, and mind to find those things that we have pushed aside or way back to protect ourselves. We often push them back as a way of developing defense mechanisms. What God has showed me through someone else is that my anger and bitterness towards my family had caused me to have a spirit of infirmity in my body. I spent one morning in retched tears and wailing asking God to uproot the bitterness towards my family. What a morning that was and when I got through, I began to be able to write this chapter!

I stand here before you today as a **HEALED** woman of God from all of my life toxins that were in my body! I'm healed from the hurt, pain, guilt and rejection. I can now go forth in the work of the Lord for the Kingdom. I can now tell my story of how God came, healed, delivered and took me through some of the darkest months of my life in order to have a testimony to share with someone.

God has not only been healing me but my son has also been healed. My son had a rough middle school experience after he left the 5th grade at East Elementary where his favorite teacher taught. She pushed and encouraged my son harder than any of his teachers in the past or in middle school. She prepared him for his middle school experience the best she could. But he had several hard tests and trials he had to endure and me along with him. As a mother it's hard to watch your child go from a very open and outspoken person to a closed off and introverted person. But in the last 60 days I saw God do amazing things with the gifted and brilliant mind He's given him. I saw God take this young man and give him a great ability to design and write programs for two Robots. Then, on May 18, 2017 @ 10 a.m. I saw God give him the release and healing he needed. The talkative, outspoken and humorous young man that I knew was back with a vengeance. His whole atmosphere changed after he had officially finished with middle school.

So when God starts healing you he doesn't just heal you. He also begins to heal those around you. He begins to do new things in your household, life naturally & spiritually, and at your job and church. I wouldn't change anything for this journey of healing that God has put me on starting from January 2017 until now. Has it been easy? NO! Has it been painful at times? YES! But has it been worth it? OH YES IT HAS!

The joy of Healing

Renewed and Refreshed

Chapter 10: The Ministry

On December 17, 2016 during my prayer time God gave me the name of a ladies ministry called War Room Warriors Ladies Ministry. God told me the purpose of this ministry is to teach ladies how to pray and become prayer warriors and war with their hands. On February 4, 2017 God had me to hold the first ladies' bible study.

I have watched God transform two specific young ladies who were ever so thirsty and hungry for God's word. They both have strong prayer lives and personal relationships with him. Has it been easy for them? No not always they can tell you that. Has God been blessing them (yes he has!) abundantly.

They are much stronger than they were when we started in February 2017. I'm not the same person either and I'm much stronger than I was then as well.

God has a plan, journey, destiny and purpose for my life. Will it always be easy? No it won't but I know with God it will all be possible and work out for my good. I pray every day for God to keep me humble and a blessing to his kingdom. I pray he continues to grace me in teaching ladies, teenage girls and young girls how to pray. I pray God continues to grace me as a prayer warrior and to war with their hands and have a personal relationship with God.

God knew that in order to have the foundation necessary for me I needed specific parents to raise me. I needed my aunt and uncle to raise me. I needed to be in a Christian home with two parents that loved me. I needed to be raised on a foundation of prayer, reading the word, fasting and having a relationship with God. I needed parents that could love me unconditionally for all I would go through. God knew I needed someone to show me an example of a mother who sacrificed for their child. I needed an example of a minister who not only accepted the call but lived the life of a minister. I needed parents that would lead by example. God knew I would need a mother who was a woman of God who led her Christian walk by example. In the ministry I now lead, I teach other women how to pray and have a relationship with God. I teach and lead them how to allow God to be their foundation. I teach them how to use their arsenal. God spoke to me that some of the women have attempted suicide in their pass. At times I was led to minister to those women and now I share my story. I know I am a suicide survivor because of the medicine I took. God told me he spared my life. He told me that death is not what I ultimately wanted. I just wanted to stop hurting.

I am also a survivor of two abusive relationships. I was in an abusive relationship where I was being sexually abused. I was also in another relationship where I was being physically abused. I was also challenged with the decision of do I stay and protect my child so we can be together? Or do I kill you and my child becomes an orphan because one parent tried to defend their life form being killed by the other parent? I made a decision for the safety, sanity and peace of me and my child to leave. We stayed in a shelter for one week. So ladies, if you feel like you have no place to go there is always the place to go. Don't risk your life because you make an excuse to stay.

I teach the women in my ministry about having a prayer life. I teach them necessary Christian principles and responsibilities. I encourage them that although they may have obstacles, challenges and you have people praying with you and for you, they will not take your foolishness. They will hold you accountable.

I know that I am doing what God has purposed for me to do. However, I have just scratched the surface of what he called me to do. He wants his daughters to be warriors in prayer. I am doing all that my mom taught me to do and was an example of in ministry. Looking from where I am now and what has happened is amazing. When these ladies come to the other side of all that has been done, these women are going to be looking for something and I have to be prepared to give them Christ.

Scriptures that God loves me:
1 Corinthians 13:13
Jeremiah 31:3
John 15:13
John 3:16
John 15:9
1 John 4:19
1 John 4:16
1 John 3:1
1 John 4:8
Lamentations 3:22-23
Psalm 103:8
Psalm 136:26
Psalm 63:3
Psalm 86:15
Romans 5:8
The following pages are picture of War Room Warriors Ladies Ministry in action.

Ministry Logo

Ministry

Conclusion

This is what God gave me to give you today. No matter what you've been through or go through in life, God has written each and every one of our futures already. So, we are just living out what He's already written for us. This is true because *in Jeremiah 1:5*

"Before I formed you in the womb I knew you; Before you were born I sanctified you;
I ordained you a prophet to the nations." and
"Jeremiah 29:11 For I know the thoughts that I think toward you, says the LORD, thoughts of peace and not of evil, to give you a future and a hope."

God wrote our future before we were even formed in our mother's womb. He already knew what roads we were going to take and how it would all turn out when we took those roads. So, NOTHING that we do or go through catches God by surprise you know why?

Because He knows our future for He is the author of it. I pray that God has blessed you to see the transformation that He has done in my life. My only regret is that my mom didn't live to see it here on earth. I do believe that she's smiling down on me from heaven.

I stand before you as a once broken woman of God that is now a HEALED woman of God ready to do God's Kingdom work that He's called me to do!

About the author

Minister Sonja Walker is a ministerial leader with a strong apostolic and prophetic intercessory call on her life. She is a mother, daughter and friend to many. Minister Sonja was raised in a solid Christian home where she developed a foundation and walk with Christ. She is a tenured employee for the state of Missouri of twenty years. She is both a hearer and doer of the word. She is the founder and leader of War Room Warriors Ministry. God called her to birth this ministry in 2017 in order to teach and train women in the area of intercession, prayer, discipleship and spiritual warfare. The ministry operates as the Ms. Clara to the Elizabeths. This is demonstrated through birthing women into spiritual maturity. The ministry also functions to evangelize, encourage, strengthen, motivate and inspire women into spiritual maturity through a disciplined prayer life.

Reflections/Thoughts:

www.ingramcontent.com/pod-product-compliance
Lightning Source LLC
Chambersburg PA
CBHW071626170426
43195CB00038B/2136